My Big Handy Bible
By Cecilie Olesen
Copyright 2013 © Scandinavia Publishing House
Drejervej 15, 3rd floor
DK-2400 Copenhagen NV
Denmark
Email: info@scanpublishing.dk

Printed in China
ISBN: 9788772479934

MY FIRST portable BIBLE

text by Cecilie Olesen
Illustrations by Gustavo Mazali

scandinavia

Contents

In the beginning

In the beginning before
anything was made, there was
God. He created everything: Light
and darkness, the skies and the oceans,
all the animals and everything on earth.
Then He created Adam and Eve. God looked at all
He had created and was pleased with everything.

Genesis 1:1-31

Noah builds an ark

God saw that people in the world became very wicked, so He decided to start over again with a man called Noah. God told Noah to build an ark and bring all the different animals into the ark. It rained for many days, until the earth was complety covered by water. Then Noah sent out a dove. When it returned, with an olive leaf in its beak, Noah knew they would see land again.

Genesis 8:1-16

Tower of Babel

The people in Babel were building a tower. They wanted it to reach heaven thinking they could be as great as God. Then God made them speak different languages. Suddenly nobody understood each other and they could not finish the huge tower.

Genesis 11:1-9

A promise to Abraham

God had promised Abraham and Sarah a son, but for many years nothing happened. God was good and kept His promise when the time was right. Abraham was 100 years old when Sarah gave birth to their son. They gave him the name Isaac, it means 'he laughs'. Sarah said "God has brought me laughter".
Genesis 21:1-7

Joseph the Dreamer

Joseph was the youngest of all his brothers. One day his father Jacob gave him a fancy coat, to show that he was his favourite son and so Joseph's brothers hated him. Joseph dreamed that he one day would be greater than all his brother and rule over them. He told them about his dreams and this made his brothers so angry, they sold him to Medianite traders.

Genesis 37:5-35

14

Joseph in Egypt

In Egypt Joseph was sold as a slave, but God looked after Joseph and blessed him with a talent to interpret dreams. He even interpreted Pharaoh's own dreams. Pharaoh became very fond of Joseph and made him governor of Egypt. To prevent people from starving - Joseph stored up food in great silos. Later when a famine came he brought his father and all his brothers to live in Egypt too. Genesis 41:1- 41

Moses

Many years later a new Pharaoh ruled Egypt. He forced Jacob's descendants, the Israelites, into slavery. He ordered his soldiers to kill all their baby boys, fearing they would become too powerful. One day Pharaoh's daughter found a crying baby in a basket among the reeds in the river. The baby boy's sister, Miriam, had hid him in the reeds to protect him from the Egyptian soldiers. The princess chose to bring him up and gave him the name Moses as she said: "I have drawn him out of the water."
Exodus 2:1-10

Out of Egypt

God spoke to Moses.
He told him to lead his family
and all the Israelites out of their
slavery in Egypt. God would lead them to a new land,
the land of Canaan. On the way they had to cross the sea.
God told Moses to stretch out his staff over the water.
Then God made a strong wind blow the water away, and
the people of Israel walked on dry ground through the sea.

Exodus 14:15-16

The Ten Commandments

On the way to Canaan - the Israelites walked
through the desert. While they were there, God gave
Moses Ten Commandments carved onto two stone tablets.
The Commandments taught the Israelite people how to
serve and obey God and live in love and peace with each other.
Exodus 24:12

23

24

Jericho

In the new land, the Israelites came to the mighty city of Jericho. God told the Israelite people to march around the city once a day for six days. On the seventh day the Israelites walked around the city seven times. When the priests blew their trumpets and people shouted, the city walls fell and the Israelites were able to conquer the city. Joshua 6:1-5

Gideon

While Gideon was leader, the Israelite people were terrorized by their enemies. Gideon gathered a large army, but God told him he had too many men. Gideon trusted in God and he ended up with an army of only 300. When night came they attacked the enemy, blowing trumpets and waving torches. The enemy got so scared they ran away and Gideon won a huge victory.

Judges 7:1-67

Samson

Manoah and his wife were childless, but an angel of
the Lord appeared and said that they would have a son.
The angel also said: "No razor may be used on his head,
he will be set apart to God from birth." The boy's name
was Samson. God blessed him and made him very strong.
God used Samson to save the Israelites from their enemies.
Judges 13:1-25

28

Ruth

Ruth was a widow and lived as a foreigner in Bethlehem. She took care of her mother-in-law. Both of them were very poor. God saw her needs and gave her a husband and son; a new family to love and be loved by. Ruth 4:1-22

Samuel

As a young boy Samuel came to live in the temple where he served God. One night Samuel heard a voice and thought it was Eli, the priest calling. This happened three times. Finally Eli said to Samuel: "If it happens again, say, 'Speak, Lord, for your servant is listening'. Again God spoke: "Samuel! Samuel!" and Samuel replied as Eli had told him. Later Samuel became a judge in Israel and a mighty man for God.
1 Samuel 3:6-10

33

David

David was the youngest of eight brothers.
From childhood he worked as a shepherd.
He was brave, courageous and strong. He fought and
killed lions and bears to protect the flocks.
God talked to Samuel and asked him to go and
anoint David to be King of Israel.
1. Samuel 16:13

David and Goliath

The Philistines and the Israelites gathered their armies for war. One of the Philistines was a giant called Goliath. Everyday he boastet and shouted bad things about God and Israel. All the Israelites were afraid of him.

When David
heard what Goliath said he
got so angry that he went out
to fight him with the firm belief that God
would be with him. With one stone from
his sling shot David killed Goliath.

1 Samuel 17:11

King Solomon

Salomon was the son of David. When David was old he announced Solomon King in his place. Salomon loved the Lord and walked in His ways. One night the Lord said to Salomon: "Ask for whatever you want me to give you." He asked for wisdom to govern the people and wisdom to know the difference between right and wrong. Solomon's wish pleased God so much He blessed him with both wisdom and wealth. People came from all over the world to listen to Solomon's wisdom.

1. Kings 3:5-14

Elijah

God wanted to prove that He was the only God. He told Elijah to challenge the priests of the false god Baal. Two alters were built, one for Baal and one for God.

Elijah said: "You call on the name of your god, and I'll call on the Lord. The god who answers with fire – he is God." For many hours the prophets of Baal shouted and danced, but nothing happened. When Elijah prayed to God – God sent a violent fire and the people of Israel praised the Lord as God.
1. Kings 18:38

41

Elisah and Naaman

The commander of the Syrian army, Naaman, suffered from leprosy. A young servant girl from Israel suggested that he should visit the prophet in Samaria. Naaman believed her and went to see the prophet Elisah. Elisah's servant told Naaman to go and dip himself seven times in the Jordan river. That really angered Naaman, but in the end he did it and was completely healed.

2. Kings 5:14

Nehemiah

Nehemiah heard that the enemy had destroyed the wall that protected Jerusalem. He wanted to rebuild it, so the city could be safe and whole again. While some were building others stood guard so their enemies could not stop their work.
Nehemiah 3:17

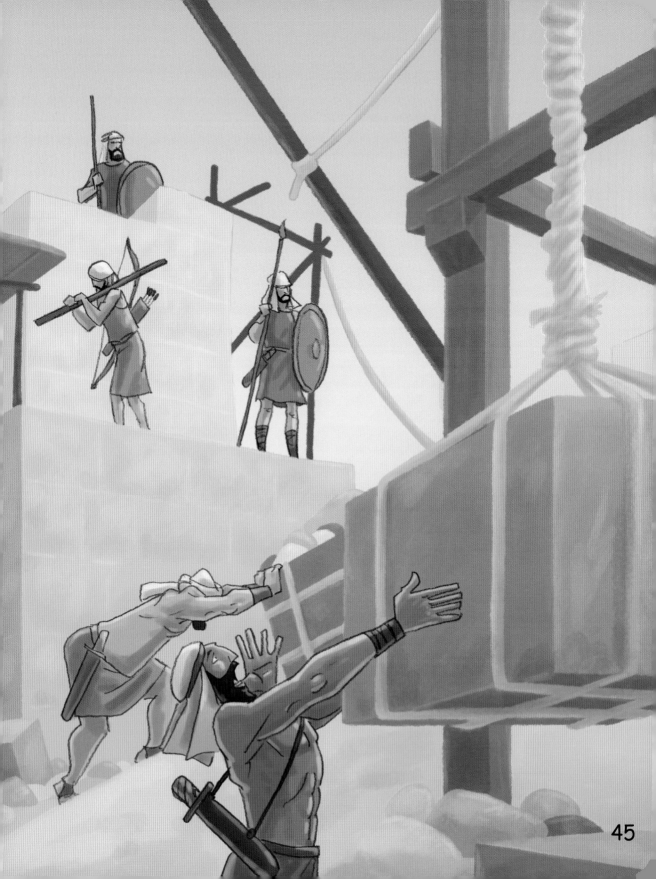

45

Esther

Esther was an Israelite and had also become queen of Persia. When she heard that her people were in peril, she risked her life by approaching the king uninvited. Esther trusted in God and asked the king to save her people. The king was happy to see her and held out his scepter to her – and the people were saved.

Esther 5:2

Psalms

The psalms were written as prayers to God.
They show what God is like. Psalm 23 is written
by King David and tells us that God cares for us
always, that he never leaves us, but blesses us
with everything good.

The Fiery Furnace

The Babylonian King Nebuchadnezzar was furious with rage because Daniel's three friends refused to worship the image of gold that he had set up. The three friends only wanted to serve God, therefore the king had them thrown into an incredible hot furnace. Amazed was the king when he saw them walking around inside the oven with another person who looked like a son of gods. This was an angel God had sent to save them from the flames.

Daniel 3:25

51

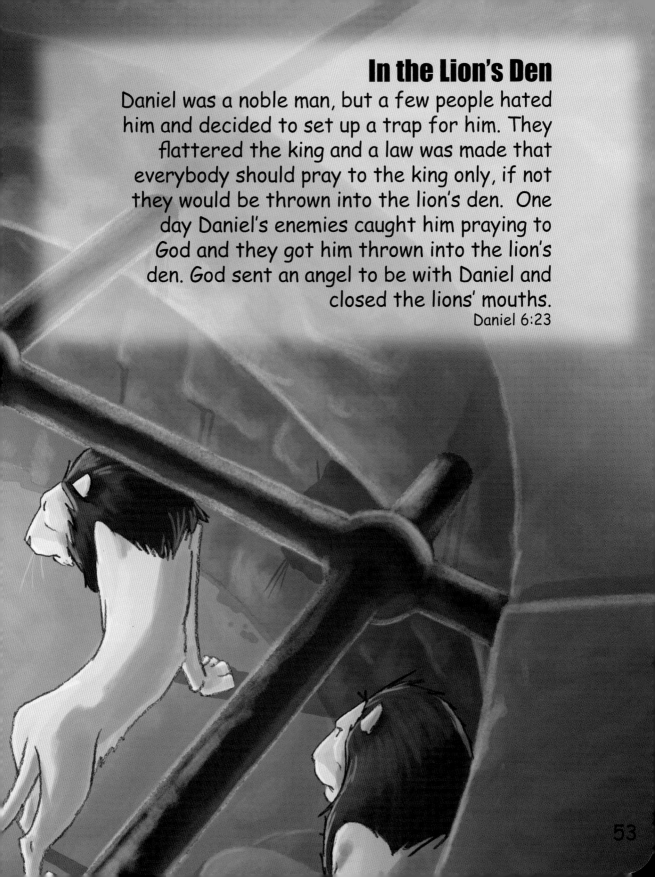

In the Lion's Den

Daniel was a noble man, but a few people hated him and decided to set up a trap for him. They flattered the king and a law was made that everybody should pray to the king only, if not they would be thrown into the lion's den. One day Daniel's enemies caught him praying to God and they got him thrown into the lion's den. God sent an angel to be with Daniel and closed the lions' mouths.

Daniel 6:23

53

Jonah

People in Nineveh were very evil. God told Jonah to go there and tell them to live good lives. But Jonah was afraid to do so and sailed away to hide from God.
God sent a storm and Jonah was thrown into the sea.

A big fish
swallowed him
and spat him out
on the beach. Then
Jonah went to Nineveh.
The people listened to
him and stopped doing
wicked things.
Jonah 1:17

The birth of Jesus

Mary was engaged to Joseph and travelled with him to Bethlehem. She was soon going to have a baby, and while they were there, she gave birth to her first-born Son. She dressed Him in baby clothes and laid Him on a bed of hay, because there was no room for them in the inn. An angel told shepherds in the fields about the newborn King and they hurried off to find Him.

Luke 2:5-17

57

58

Jesus in the temple

When Jesus was 12 years old He went to Jerusalem with his parents to celebrate Easter. Jesus stayed in the temple and spoke with the priests. They were all very surprised that Jesus knew so much about God and His Word. His parents could not find Jesus and searched for three days until they finally found Him in the temple. Luke 2:46

Jesus preaches

Jesus told people how much God loved them. He taught them what it means to be good and love others. He said: "blessed are the pure in heart, and blessed are the peacemakers." He chose twelve men, they became his disciples.
Luke 5:1-11

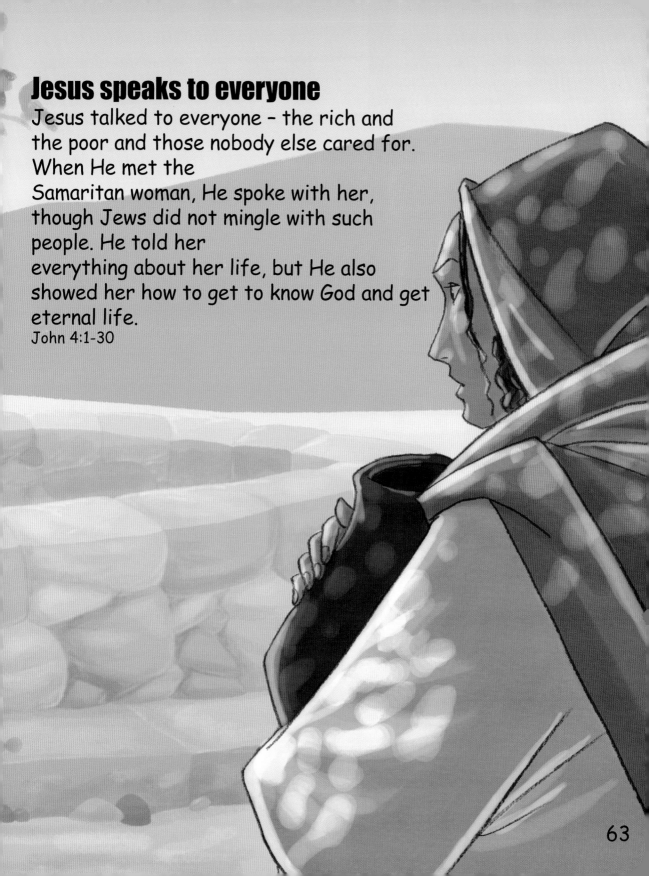

Jesus speaks to everyone

Jesus talked to everyone – the rich and the poor and those nobody else cared for. When He met the Samaritan woman, He spoke with her, though Jews did not mingle with such people. He told her everything about her life, but He also showed her how to get to know God and get eternal life.

John 4:1-30

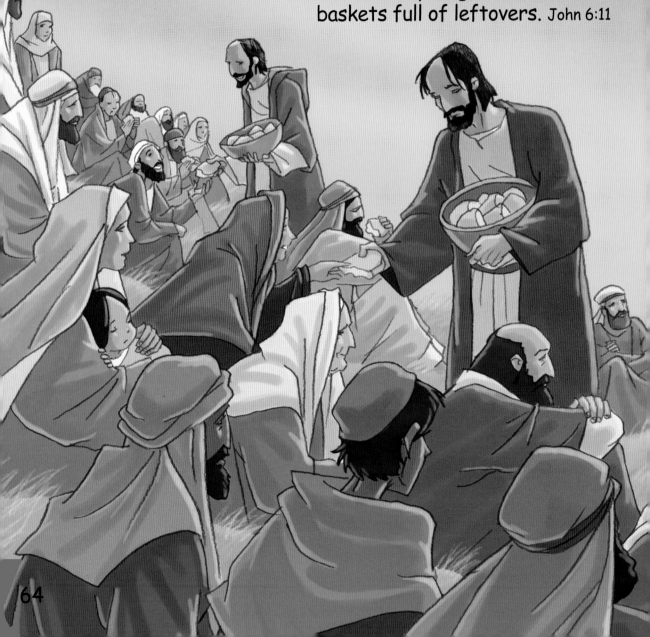

Jesus feeds the hungry

Jesus worked many miracles. One day He preached to five thousand people. After a long time they got very hungry, but they did not know where to get food from. A boy brought five loaves of bread and two fish. Jesus blessed the food and everybody had plenty to eat. After the meal, the disciples gathered several baskets full of leftovers. John 6:11

The good shepherd

Jesus talked in parables so everybody could understand Him, when He shared his knowledge about the Kingdom of God. Jesus said that He was like a good shepherd and we were like the sheep. If the good shepherd lost a sheep He would search until He found it and celebrate it with all His friends.

Luke 15:3-6

Peter walks on the water

The disciples were in a boat on a lake in stormy weather. Suddenly Jesus came walking on the water. The disciples were terrified. But Peter shouted, "Lord, if it's you, tell me to come to you on the water." Jesus replied: "Come." So Peter stepped out of the boat and walked towards Jesus. Soon Peter got scared looking at the waves and he started sinking. Jesus reached out, pulled him up and saved him.

Matthew 14:27-31

Jesus meets Zacchaeus

Zacchaeus was a tax collector and people did not like him because he cheated. One day when Jesus was passing through the town, Zacchaeus, being of short stature, climbed a tree just to catch a glimpse of Him. Jesus passed by the tree, looked up and said: "Zacchaeus, come down, I must stay at your house today." He came down at once and welcomed him gladly.
Luke 19:5

71

Jesus blessed the children

Some people brought their children to Jesus,
so that he could place his hands on them and pray for them.
His disciples told the people to stop bothering
him. But Jesus said, "Let the children come to me,
don't try to stop them! People who are like these
children belong to God's kingdom."
Matthew 18:1-14

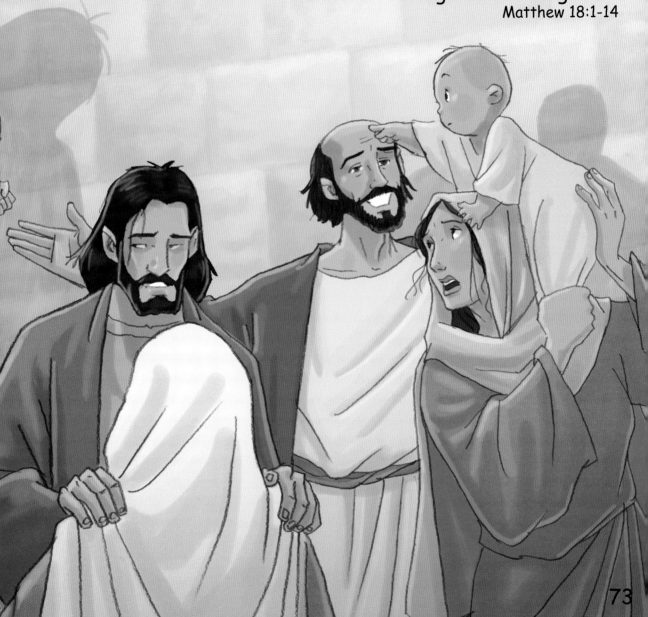

73

The last supper

Jesus knew that He would soon return to his Father in Heaven. He had planned a last dinner with His disciples. At this dinner, Jesus told them always to remember Him when they shared the bread and the wine. With sadness he told the 12 disciples that one of them would betray him. They all became sad.
Luke 22:14-22

Jesus dies

Jesus was loved by the people, but the leaders in Israel hated him because He told people that the teachings of the leaders were in error. The religious leaders brought Jesus before the judge and even though he didn't find Him guilty of anything, the religious leaders roused the crowds to yell, "Kill Him, kill Him. Nail Him to a cross!" And so it happened Jesus was crucified.

Luke 23:33

The resurrection

Early in the morning on the third day after the crucifixion,
Mary Magdalene and other women came to visit Jesus' grave. They
were met by an angel who told them Jesus had risen from the
dead. Later Jesus met the disciples and commanded them to tell all
people about Him. Before He was taken up into heaven, He prayed
for his disciples and all people who one day would believe in Him.
Matthew 28:1-20

In Jesus' footsteps

After Jesus had returned to
Heaven, the disciples began to
speak and teach about Jesus.
They followed Jesus' example
and went out to heal the sick and
brought relief to suffering people.
Acts 3:1-10